A TRICK OF SUNLIGHT

T0096807

A TRICK OF SUNLIGHT

POEMS

Dick Davis

Swallow Press / Ohio University Press
Athens

Swallow Press / Ohio University Press, Athens, Ohio 45701
www.ohio.edu/oupress

© 2006 by Dick Davis

Printed in the United States of America
All rights reserved

Swallow Press / Ohio University Press books are printed on acid-free paper ⊗ ™

14 13 12 11 10 09 08 07 06   5 4 3 2 1

Library of Congress Cataloging-in-Publication Data
Davis, Dick, 1945–
   A trick of sunlight : poems / Dick Davis.
     p. cm.
   ISBN-13: 978-0-8040-1088-7 (alk. paper)
   ISBN-10: 0-8040-1088-9 (alk. paper)
   ISBN-13: 978-0-8040-1089-4 (pbk. : alk. paper)
   ISBN-10: 0-8040-1089-7 (pbk. : alk. paper)
   I. Title

PR 6054.A8916T75 2006
821'.914—dc22

                              2005035931

Acknowledgments

Some of the poems in this book have appeared in the following publications:
The Atlanta Literary Review ("Cythère," "Hérédia"), *The Owl* ("On a Remark of
Karl Kraus," "Author, Translator . . ."), *Parnassus* ("Listening"), *Fashioned Pleasures*
("The Old Model's Advice to the New Model"), and *The New Criterion* ("A Mystery
Novel," "Before Sleep," "Shopping").

   Nine poems included here ("Pasts," "Turgeniev and Friends," "Driving West-
ward," "Water," "Chèvrefeuille," "Edgar," "Under $6 a Bottle," "Happiness," "Get-
ting Away") appeared in the online journal *The New Compass*.

CONTENTS

A TRICK OF SUNLIGHT

"The heart has its abandoned mines . . ."
Old workings masked by scrub and scree.
Sometimes, far, far beneath the surface
An empty chamber will collapse;
But to the passerby the change
Is almost imperceptible:
A leaf's slight tremor, or a stone
Dislodged into the vacant shaft.

Chèvrefeuille

In a neglected glade
The hazel sapling's shade
Quickens with early spring:
New tendrils clutch and cling—
A honeysuckle twines
Its tentative thin vines
Reaching now in, now out,
Above, below, about,
Till intricate, strong strands
Clasp like a myriad hands.
Love's leaves and limbs conspire
As if unsaid desire
Could intimately tether
Their substances together
And none could separate
Their growths' complicit state.
Bright in the summer sun
Two tangled lives are one.

Getting Away

Once, when I was a child of seven or eight,
I turned a corner on a wooded path
And saw a fox a few feet from my face.
We stood stock-still and took each other in:
Instinctively, I looked down at his paws;
He stared at me a moment, then he turned
And loped away downhill, between the trees,
Unhurried, but inexorably gone.

His paws had all been there, I'd counted them,
And so he couldn't be *that* fox, the fox
Some serious grown-up had described for me,
The one whose inadvertent paw had stepped
On steel that sprang shut, snap (the man had snapped
His fingers), just like this: he gripped my arm,
Then asked how brave I was. Could I have done
What that fox did? He'd gnawed the fur and flesh
Down to the bone, imagine how that hurt,
Then cracked the bone, chewed through the lot, and so
Escaped, leaving the keeper only this:
And here he'd slipped a paw into my hand,
Soft, small, and lifeless, with no blood on it.

There was another story I was told
Around that time, which in my mind belonged
With that hallucinatory, bad moment.
The village churchyard had an ancient grave

Whose slab had moved, so that a gap had opened
Through which the darkness showed. One moonless night
A group of scallywags had dared each other
To run and put a hand beneath the slab.
One had agreed, and, as the others waited
Crouched down beside the churchyard wall, they'd heard
A terror-stricken scream, and run off home.
The next day their companion was discovered:
When he had turned to join his friends, a branch
Had snagged his jersey's sleeve, as if a hand
Reached out to hold him, and his heart had stopped.

The fox then or the boy: which would I be?

Water

Stirred by the charm and beauty of your voice
I lost for moments at a time your meaning:
My mind reached back some thirty years to where
A small stream pulsed between Italian rocks.
High somewhere in the Apennines I saw
Clear water bubbling from an unseen source:
Light glinted on it like a minor blessing,
An inexhaustible sweet iridescence—
Redundant beauty spilling endlessly,
That in another form I drink from now.

Happiness

The weirdest entry in our lexicon,
The word whose referent we never know—
A river valley from a Book of Hours
Somewhere in southern Europe long ago.

Or once, to someone walking by the Loire,
A trick of sunlight on a summer's day
Revealed the Virgin in rococo clouds:
The peasants in the fields knelt down to pray.

Hérédia

French was his mother's voice, sweet, close and warm,
Muffling the Spanish of their vast estate—
Their backwater baroquely out of date,
Time's flotsam from a long-forgotten storm.
Latin and Greek sustained him through the swarm
Of present truths his heart could not translate.
Paris would distance them: there the debate
Would poise contingency against pure form.

Paris returns the febrile compliment
And her Academician seeks the sea;
Sated with Rome and with the orient
He walks the barren cliffs of Brittany,
Gazing across the formless waves to where
The huge sun sinks beyond Cape Finistère.

The Man from Provins

(as related in Joinville's chronicle of the crusade of Louis IX)

After Damietta fell, I pitied them
As one might pity any wretched prisoners;
I saw too what I'd been, friendless and filthy,
Emaciated, sick, a foolish failure.

My friends said I should parley with their king
And though I was concerned I'd jeopardize
The life I've built up here, a kind of guilt,
Or curiosity, or something worse,
Persuaded me to be their dragoman.
You should have seen their faces when my voice
Betrayed that I was French like them, or had been.

I don't know what I'd hoped for. What I got
Was royal anger and a show of horror,
The usual rhetoric of new arrivals,
Made sharper by that piety of his,
Of which his hangers-on are all so proud.
But holy horror's of no use to me:
I left him in his tent, relieved to stand
Back in the sunlight where a man can see things.

Then one of them, as if to make amends,
Came out, and caught my arm, and questioned me,
Eager to know exactly where I'd come from
And why I'd stayed. I told him bluntly then
I was from Provins, famous for its fairs,
A place that had been rich, a handsome town

Perched on its hill above the fertile plain,
Become a haunt of beggars and stray dogs,
No building going forward, and the young men,
Or those who had their wits about them, leaving.
Why should I long for that? I've vineyards here,
A noble house, and other men's respect,
Besides which I have now acquired two things
I love in my ungainly, foreign way:
The language of my neighbors, and a wife.

He asked me urgently about the faith
Which he insisted was still mine, or should be;
I answered him as seemed appropriate,
So that he left believing what he wished to.

Before Sleep

Let me not lie here, mulling the day's anger,
Rehearsing, if there have been such, its tears;
Let no bitterness beckon, envy linger;
Save me from Circe's, Medusa's, cruel stares.

Let me slip to Sleep's Kingdom unencumbered
By guilt I don't need, by guards who would ask me
For visas I've lost; let me enter unhindered
To where I'm at home: let no one suspect me.

May Kindness take charge then, to see that I'm dipped
In Oblivion's warm baths; and when I emerge
Let me wander Love's island, as one who's released
Unscathed from Doubt's dungeons, manumitted, at large.

The Old Model's Advice to the New Model

Artistic license isn't all it's painted:
It's true he sometimes wants to move to passion
Before you've had the time to get acquainted,
But that's just flattery or arty fashion.
Take it from me, you won't spend much time rolling
Across the floor or in his bed: his gazes
Are usually less carnal than controlling,
And after all these years what still amazes—
Well, me at least—is how what he's created
Can look like Lust Incarnate's drooling doting
And Lust is what he's certain he's defeated.
If you want that, you'll finish up with nothing.
It's painting he gets off on—that's his pleasure;
He'll paint, but probably not want, your treasure.

Edgar

(i.m. Edgar Bowers, 1924–2000)

A few things that recall you to me, Edgar:

A stately '80s Buick; hearing a car
Referred to by a coaxing sobriquet—
"Now come on, Captain, don't you let me down."
French spoken in a conscious southern accent;
An idiom calqued and made ridiculous
("Eh, mettons ce spectacle sur le chemin").
"Silly," dismissive in its deep contempt,
"Oh, he's a silly; an amiable silly,
But still a silly." Or the words I first
Encountered in your captious conversations,
"Tad," "discombobulated," "catawampus."
The usage that you gave me once for "totaled"—
"Oh cruel fair, thy glance hath totaled me."

Most recently, in Cleveland's art museum,
The French medieval tapestries brought back
Your unabashed reaction to their beauty,
And how, for once, you'd stood there almost speechless,
Examining Time's Triumph inch by inch,
Enraptured by its richness, by the young man
Proud in his paradisal place, until
You saw what his averted gaze avoided—
The old man, beaten, bent double by fate's blows,
Driven from youth's charmed, evanescent circle:
And how you'd wanted to be sure I'd seen him.

Listening

Sweet Reason rules the morning—what's as sweet as
Rosalyn Tureck playing Bach partitas?

Midday's for Haydn, who loved everyone
(Except that pompous pig Napoleon)—
Music's Hippocrates ("First do no harm"),
An *Aufklärung* of common sense and charm.

Mozart and Schubert own the afternoon—
High spirits and a Fiordiligi swoon;
A sudden key change: you will die alone.
The shadow that you stare at is your own.

Then comes the night. Pandora's lid is lifted,
Each scene implodes before it can be shifted—
Longing's a tenor's accurate bravura,
Sex and Despair are *Fach* and *Tessitura:*

And heaven's where the mind's sopranos sing
In harmonies undreamt of in *The Ring.*

What I Think

On your advice I saw a shrink
Which did me no damn good at all.
She seemed to be the missing link.

I thought she'd calm me, help me think,
And be the David to my Saul . . .
On your advice I saw a shrink;

Substantial as a tiddlywink
Her IQ was Neanderthal,
She seemed to be the missing link.

I thought we'd iron out a kink
Or two, or fight, or have a ball,
(On your advice I saw a shrink);

Perhaps, once, she was on the brink
Of saying something sensible . . .
But no, she was the missing link.

Blandly we skated round the rink,
And didn't jump, and didn't fall.
On your advice I saw a shrink
But didn't find the missing link.

The Scholar as a Naughty Boy

Conceive of history as a crumbling palace
Run by a lord both arbitrary and callous;

A little boy peers down between the banisters
And lobs imaginary teargas canisters

Then pokes about in semi-Stygian gloom
Ransacking treasures in the lumber room;

Scuffed velvet, shattered ormolu, stained pages;
The cast-off junk and wisdom of the ages.

Bats flitter, vermin litter, spiders skitter;
Down there the statesmen coruscate and glitter.

Anglais Mort à Santa Barbara

Rejoicing in his accent (oh he could sweetly coo it,
And charm the wealthy widows, and didn't mind who knew it)—
They said he went to England, every summer, to renew it.

As never-to-be-vulgar was his peculiar vulgarity
His manners caused his cronies much behind-his-back hilarity,
But as he's gone for good now, why be churlish with our charity?

The morning mist burns off the shore, but this time not for him.
In darkness he is lying still. His eyes, forever dim,
Cannot peruse his Betjeman, or favorite Barbara Pym.

The Skeptic

The people who discuss their other lives
Are utterly unfazed by questions like
"But where do all the extra souls appear from?"
They mutter something about animals,
And quickly change the subject to the fact
That they were once the Empress Josephine,
Or Balzac, or the best friend of St. Thecla.

Small children with a box of dress-up clothes
Enthusiastically try on new lives:
The princess and the pirate preen themselves
Before their gesturing peers, all glamorous,
All brave and loved, their rags turned into riches.
There's always one who gets a little wistful,
Tearful even, unsure what he should wear.
Occasionally, there'll be a thorough skeptic
Who simply takes his clothes off, and puts none on.

Driving

Driving in rush hour traffic
I saw behind the wheel
Of a car hurtling straight at me
The face of my friend Patrick

Who died twenty years ago
Driving in rush hour traffic,
And I was so afraid
To see those eyes that I

Was sure were his fix mine
That for a moment I
Lost all control, and almost
Did as he did years ago.

Do you remember those few hours we spent
Enchanted by the pictures at the Frick?

Whole rooms—thank God!—abandoned to mere charm,
To versions of *douceur* and dignity

(As if the two of them encompassed all
That might be said of life without a shudder);

And in the atrium the fountain plashing,
The almost silence, and the little frog.

Then, as we stepped outside, the swirling snow.

Flying Back

The airport's cluttered lounge presents
The usual mob of miscreants—
The loud, the ugly, and the stupid,
The sad sacks never blessed by Cupid:
But I can't hate the human zoo,
I'll soon be flying back to you.

The conversations swirl around me,
Elsewhere I know they would have drowned me—
But let them prattle, let them chatter,
Nothing they say will ever matter—
I bless the whole loquacious crew,
And think of flying back to you.

The screaming infant, and the bore
Who's got the skinny on the war,
The cell-phone junkie, and the jerk
Who tells me how tax shelters work
I love them all, I really do,
I'm flying back, right now, to you.

And in the plane I'm sat beside
Some fat fanatic Woe-Betide
Who tells me in great detail why
Sinners like me are damned . . . but I
Just nod and murmur "Whoop-de-do,"
Happily flying back to you.

This airline ought to be unlawful,
The flight's delayed, the food is awful,
The stolid stewardess ignores me,
I've brought the wrong book and it bores me—
But I'm not mad or sad or blue . . .
Because I'm flying back to you.

Three Emilys

For Emily Grosholz

An adolescent solipsist, I clung to
The law laid down in Haworth parsonage;
I knew the empty uplands you had sung to
And took your tempests as my heritage.
I grew into the world, and came to learn
That one can sing but also think and speak;
Amherst had spoken once, and I would earn
The right to be as accurate and oblique.
Now the world's here; there's nowhere else to go to.
Dear Emily, your gentle words have shown
Here is the truth the winds of childhood blow to,
Its beauty and its horror are our own:
Here is the happiness and grief we grow to,
The shared sweet world, in which we are alone.

Turgeniev and Friends

Trained by a brutal father, they became
The divas Malibran and Viardot;
The techniques they had mastered blow by blow
Divided Paris with their florid fame.
Meanwhile, in Oryel, a young mother beat
Her whimpering child to make a man of him;
In time he would become a synonym
For all that's empathetic and discreet.

He fell in love with Viardot, whose spouse
Was understanding, and seemed not to mind;
They lived *à trois*, three mutually kind,
Concerned companions in a single house.
They must have traded stories, but who knows
If their compulsions ever came to blows?

Under $6 a Bottle

Shun Chardonnay—the bottle might be pretty,
But its bouquet's distinctly eau-de-kitty

Be wary of Bordeaux, which Brits call "claret"—
Imagine a metallic-tasting carrot

Watch out for anything that fizzes—Asti
Spumante is spectacularly nasty

Avoid Shiraz—there's nothing subtly Persian
About the blatant blowsy Aussie version

Don't risk the Riesling—not, that is, unless you
Know alcoholic Kool-Aid won't distress you

Choose nothing then, put all your icky picks back,
And cross the aisle to buy a Miller six-pack.

"They are not long, the days of wine and roses . . ."

I think it was the Parthians
Who first homed in on wine and roses
As *sine quibus non* when we
Discuss the good life and its pleasures.

Almost erased by history,
A shadow behind texts, a few
Prosaic ruins, enigmatic
Statues, a derisive catchphrase . . .

But still, that's quite a legacy.

Shopping

Was there a special Mess you had in mind, sir?
If you could be a little more specific . . .
As you can see we've every size and kind, sir,
From In Your Face to Mildly Soporific.

Adultery is very popular—
It's our perennial favorite, you could say:
The Shocking Pink? Most customers prefer
Discreeter models, like this Sordid Grey.

Self-Poisonings are on sale, and very buyable:
We stock *Old Fogey's Alcoholic Haze,*
The Sixties' Acid Test, and this reliable
La Mode Cocaine; it's ultrachic these days.

Loony obsessions can be quite attractive—
Religious Manias are on that wall,
They come in Solitary or Interactive;
Some say they make the biggest Mess of all.

There's Basic Selfishness, a classic line,
And always guaranteed to stay in style;
I know I couldn't function without mine—
It makes a Mess that's wonderfully worthwhile.

Still not convinced? A canny customer!
I've one more product that might interest you:
This cut-price Boredom is a beauty, sir—
And it'll do what all the others do.

Chagrin

In middle age, to my chagrin I find
That death and sex preoccupy my mind.
When de la Mare was gravely ill a kind
Friend asked if there were things for which he pined—
Flowers, say? Or fruit? Politely he declined:
"Too soon for flowers, too late for fruit." Behind
His wit my past and prospects are defined.

Pasts

The past's quaint versions of the past delight
Our tolerance with gauche anachronisms:
Ovid is *fin amor* plus archaisms,
Swooning Lucretia's stays are laced too tight,
Great Alexander is a Christian knight.
We patronize their pretty solecisms,
And even envy the distorting prisms
That bathed their pasts in such familiar light.

We're too aware to do that now, we say,
Too conscience-stricken, too sophisticated,
Although we know our empathies betray
Our own impedimenta half-translated,
And someone will be tickled pink one day
To come across the pasts that we've created.

A Visit to Grandmother's

For CT, who told me this story

When shampoo stung her eyes
Her anguished bathroom cries
Of "Oh" and "Oooh" and "Ah"
Were heard by grandmamma
As something else completely.
Later she said, discreetly,
"Lovely to hear your noise:
A young girl who enjoys
Her body won't need boys."

Can We?

Can we convincingly pretend,
And not to others but ourselves,
That we are happy? And if we could,
Would that mean that we were, pro tem,
Uncomplicatedly, just that,
Happy? And what would that be like?
The mind runs through its obvious
Loved carnal candidates . . . Well, maybe.
But probably it would resemble

Less some celestial debauch
With someone quite phenomenal
Than being in a symphony
By Haydn: having all of it—
It doesn't matter much which one—
The whole ebullient edifice,
Just there, available and real,
Impossibly to hand, forever.

Cythère

Though we can start with Botticelli—
The blonde hair streaming, and the eyes
Fixed in provocative surprise,
Her hand strategic on her belly—

Your avatars dissolve and morph;
Flesh volatized to soul, the whore
Whose flesh is cash and something more,
Punk wraith, unwieldy Willendorf,

The skinny-dipper at Lake Tahoe,
The floating world, *la belle poitrine*
Of a long-dead Minoan queen,
The plenitude of Khajuraho . . .

But now, for me, you coalesce
As French, immediate, medieval,
Making improbably coeval
Iseut, Watteau, *Bonjour Tristesse*.

I see you now, your body bare
And welcoming, your eyes intense
With passionate intelligence.
Your hands in mine, adored Cythère.

Young Scholar

She puts aside a rival's tome
(*Amor de lonh*, or mythic Rome).

Time for her bath (it's after seven),
And Renée Fleming storming heaven:

She's here to heal: to slough away
The crude detritus of the day.

A sip of wine; the recognition
That what she is is her decision.

Mind makes its peace; the mind's her home.
Cleansed now, she rises from the foam.

Farsighted

Being farsighted means
You can't make out the scenes

Happening before your eyes—
They come as a surprise.

The more remote the view
The more it speaks to you.

And clearly you can't read
That horrid snakelike screed

The world delights to call
The writing on the wall.

On a Remark of Karl Kraus

("All right, we can sleep together, but no intimacy!")

His paradox
No longer shocks;
It's just a fact now,
The way we act now.

We use, are used,
And disabused
Find coupling hateful.
Karl Kraus, be grateful

For old complexes:
Who says no sex is
The worst or only
Way to be lonely?

I lay down in the darkness of my soul
And knew that I was neither sick nor whole,
That lack defined me, and my absent presence
Was not contingent to me, but my essence.

Preferences

To my surprise
I've come to realize
I don't like poetry

(Dear, drunkly woozy,
Accommodating floozy
That she's obliged to be,

Poor girl, these days).
No, what I love and praise
Is not damp poetry

But her pert, terse,
Accomplished sibling: verse.
She's the right girl for me.

Small Talk

Not-Waking

Sleep is the happy lover who
Has no desire to let you go.

"Stay in my arms," she says, "Don't move.
Lie still, and be assured of love."

Imitatio

Our lives are calques of others' lives:
The metaphor is what survives.
Role-play, soothsay, then tell me who
You think you are when you are you.

"Live all you can; it's a mistake not to"

Of course, to recognize
This quote, and more, its truth
Means your myopic youth
Was spent quite otherwise.

Magic

I can imagine someone knowing you,
Turning the pages of the O.E.D.
And carefully cutting out the words that mean
"Goodbye," "Farewell," so you could never say them,
Then inking over all the words that mean
"Anguish," "Grief," "Loss," so he could never see them.

Soteriological

To make another person your salvation
Is to be doubly sure of your damnation.

"Interpretation is the revenge of the intellect upon art"

Dead authors are the easiest to bully,
And few enough will take them at their word:
"We must, if we're to understand X fully, . . ."
X marks the spot where parricide occurred.

Author, Translator . . .

Author, translator; now their voices switch.
Ventriloquist and doll; but which is which?

Damnation à la Mode

The various martyrdoms' ungodly promises
Ensure damnation to all doubting Thomases.

But let them preach their millenarian premises;
Eros and alcohol remain my nemeses.

Finding

We find that we outgrow, and are outgrown,
And end where we departed from, alone.

There

Absence becomes unbearable: old men
Spell out the scriptures from a distant childhood.
I shall be one of them I know, despite
The incredulity of some I pray for.

Acculturation

"This was our life," the parents said,
"The moral, only, life—so follow it."
But long before the fools were dead
They saw the children wouldn't swallow it.

Spleen

How did it happen that life didn't happen,
That nothing turned out the way it was meant to—
That though we set sail for the Fortunate Isles
Cape Disappointment's the landfall we're sent to?

The Phoenix

Gold against blue, the fabled phoenix flies,
A mote borne upward by obscure desire—
A sudden signature of lambent fire
Glimpsed for a moment in the spirit's skies.

But look, the cynosure of wondering eyes
Descends and labors, huge now, a machine
That Leonardo might have dreamed he'd seen
Beating its creaking vans through Tuscan skies;

An artifice of grief that cannot rise,
A Hindenburg of hope, whose flagrant crash
We flinch from, breathing Pentecostal ash
As motes swirl upward to uncertain skies.

Dis's Defense

Now that you've heard the prosecution's case
You think I haven't got a leg to stand on:
"How dare that senile death's-head lay a hand on
Our pretty paragon of youth and grace,
And drag her down to such a dismal place?"
But hold off on the verdict that you've planned on
Until you've heard my side. Let's not abandon
The court's proceedings now, *in medias res.*

Granted, she didn't want to come at first,
But she got used to it, and she's a queen there.
How can you claim my country is "accursed"
When you admit that none of you has been there?
And every single time I've set her free
Eight months go by, and she comes back to me.

William MacGonagall Welcomes the Initiative for a Greater Role for Faith-Based Education

Oh for the pure Intellectual Fever
Of Halal Madrasseh and Kosher Yeshiva

Where every last pupil's exactly like you
And with only one Answer it *has* to be true

Oh for the play of Disinterested Mind
The impartial inquiry you're certain to find

Where a Catholic Priest can tell you what's what
And ensure that you never encounter a Prot

Where a Protestant Elder can call you to order
And assure you the Pope should be swimming in ordure

Oh for the stirring, sanguinary stories
That admonish us all with Our Martyrs' past glories

Oh for the splendors of Faith-Based Education
That spread Fear and Hatred throughout the whole Nation.

William Morris

Dyeing Topsy, hands imbrued,
Dreams of scarlet brotherhood:

Pattern pattern all the day
Pattern beareth the bell away.

Dante Gabriel's always there
Painting gentle Janey's hair:

Pattern pattern all the day
Pattern beareth the bell away.

Guinevere needs no defense,
Lovely Janey jumps the fence:

Pattern pattern all the day
Pattern beareth the bell away.

Kelmscott, Iceland, anti-scrape,
Can't undo pandemic rape:

Pattern pattern all the day
Pattern beareth the bell away.

All the fruit is over-ripe,
Dying Topsy sets the type:

Pattern pattern all the day
Pattern beareth the bell away.

Driving Westward

The restaurant's full, and I'm a stranger here,
But they accommodate me in a corner.
No wine list. H'm. I order local beer.
The air-conditioning's out. It's like a sauna.

The so-so food's generic U.S.-Thai,
The décor "Hollywood meets Old Siam"—
Call it the gastronomic *King and I.*
Am I still glad I stopped here? Yes I am.

A mainly student eatery it seems:
Their voices' brief collisions and collusions
Recount the cynicism of their dreams;
"But she's so full of shit!" "You mean illusions."

The waitresses are Thai; slim and aloof,
Their slight hauteur's more touching than annoying—
Self-parody perhaps, but vivid proof
That kitsch can comfort us and not be cloying.

"Did you enjoy your meal, sir?" "It was swell."
(We're in the Fifties, yes?) The place is thriving.
I tip them far too much. I wish them well:
Replete, content, I can continue driving.

Are we going the same way?

These chance encounters which
    I can't put down to chance
Leave me confused, co-opted
    In someone else's dance.

The e-mails that you send me
    Seem sober, sane, and sensible—
But twice a day's becoming
    A bit, well, indefensible.

The phone rings as I write this
    And answering it I speak
To silence—as I've done
    So many times this week:

That can't be you now, can it?
    You're such a fluent talker;
At least you were before
    You turned into my stalker.

Emblems

Wind-bowed, the peonies' fragility
But also their resilience for a while
Seem emblematic of the lovers' state;

The struggling lovers who negotiate
By stratagems, by honesty, and guile
To be what they obscurely have to be.

A Mystery Novel

Alone and diffident
You enter what is there:
The world that does not care
For your predicament,

For mysteries of who
You must become, or what
Your place is in the plot
To which you have no clue.

Turn pages; suffer time:
And, look, you are the thread
Unraveling from the dead;
The clue; the plot; the crime.

NOTES

Chèvrefeuille

The title refers to the twelfth-century poem of the same name by Marie de France, which uses honeysuckle (chèvrefeuille) and hazel growing together as emblems of the love of Tristan and Isolde.

Hérédia

José Maria de Hérédia (1842–1905) was born in Cuba; he lived in Paris for most of his life, where he was a leading member of the Parnassian group of poets, so called for their adherence to classical models. Most of his poems are sonnets, which are marked by a scrupulous formal precision united to often extravagant and highly romantic subject matter, much of it drawn from either the Roman past or mythology.

The Man from Provins

This poem is drawn from an incident briefly recounted in the memoirs of the soldier Jean, sire de Joinville, who had accompanied Louis IX of France, known as Saint Louis, on his crusade to the Holy Land (1248–54). The expedition ended in disaster when Louis's troops were besieged and then forced to surrender at Damietta in northern Egypt. They were eventually ransomed, and returned home. The man who questions the narrator of the poem, after the king has dismissed him, is Joinville himself.

The still largely medieval town of Provins lies southeast of Paris; from having been one of the most important cities in France it began to decline economically in the thirteenth century and never recovered.

The Old Model's Advice to the New Model

This was written for inclusion in *Fashioned Pleasures*, a chapbook of sonnets, by different poets, using the rhyme words of Shakespeare's Sonnet XX.

What I Think

This poem was written in response to Wendy Cope's poem of the same name in her book *If I Don't Know* (Faber, 2001).

Turgeniev and Friends

Turgeniev's mother beat him unmercifully when he was a child. The great love of his life was the French operatic mezzo-soprano Pauline Viardot, sister of the famous Malibran. The two girls had been taught to sing by their father, a notoriously violent teacher who beat his pupils, including his daughters, for even trivial mistakes.

Cythère

Although this was originally the French name for Cytherea, a mythical Island of Love, it was also used by some poets (e.g., Ronsard) for the goddess who presides there, Aphrodite. It is this latter use which is invoked in my poem.

Young Scholar

Amor de lonh, "love from afar," is the central concern of much lyrical medieval European poetry.

"Interpretation is the revenge of the intellect upon art"

The title is a remark by Susan Sontag.

Dis's Defense

Dis is the god of the underworld, Hades in Greek mythology. He captured Persephone, the daughter of Zeus, and took her down to his kingdom, where he made her his queen. She returns to the earth every year, and this marks the beginning of spring, but always returns to her consort in Hades for the winter months.

William MacGonagall Welcomes the Initiative for a Greater Role for Faith-Based Education

William MacGonagall (1825–1902) has the dubious reputation of being "the writer of the worst poetry in English." His meter is all over the place, and he never saw a sentimental commonplace he didn't feel was an admirable subject for a poem.